THE BEST NBA
SHOOTERS
OF ALL TIME

By Barry Wilner

www.abdopublishing.com

Published by Abdo Publishing, a division of ABDO, PO Box 398166,
Minneapolis, Minnesota 55439. Copyright © 2015 by Abdo Consulting
Group, Inc. International copyrights reserved in all countries. No part
of this book may be reproduced in any form without written permission
from the publisher. SportsZone™ is a trademark and logo of Abdo
Publishing.

Printed in the United States of America, North Mankato, Minnesota
042014
092014

THIS BOOK CONTAINS
RECYCLED MATERIALS

Cover Photos: Tom Strattman/AP Images (left);
Jim Mone/AP Images (right)
Interior Photos: Tom Strattman/AP Images, 1 (left), 5, 29; Jim Mone/AP
Images, 1 (right), 4; AP Images, 7, 15; Jeff Robbins/AP Images, 9; Zuma
Press/Icon SMI, 11, 21, 43; John McDonough/Icon SMI, 13, 19; Peter
Halpern/AP Images, 17; John Swart/AP Images, 23; Douglas C. Pizac/
AP Images, 25; Gloria Ferniz/AP Images, 27; Mark Duncan/AP Images,
31; Lennox McLendon/AP Images, 33; L.M. Otero/AP Images, 35; Ron
Frehm/AP Images, 37; Michael Kaiser/AP Images, 39; Beth A. Keiser/
AP Images, 41; Elise Amendola/AP Images, 45; Tom Hood/AP Images,
47; Kevork Djansezian/AP Images, 49; Gerald Herbert/AP Images, 51;
Tony Gutierrez/AP Images, 53; Sue Ogrocki/AP Images, 55; Eric Gay/AP
Images, 57; Marcio Jose Sanchez/AP Images, 59; Ross D. Franklin/AP
Images, 61

Editor: Chrös McDougall
Series Designer: Christa Schneider

Library of Congress Control Number: 2014932907

Cataloging-in-Publication Data
Wilner, Barry.
 The best NBA shooters of all time / Barry Wilner.
  p. cm. -- (NBA's best ever)
ISBN 978-1-62403-413-8
1. National Basketball Association--Juvenile literature. 2. Shooters
(Basketball)--Juvenile literature. I. Title.
796.323--dc23

2014932907

TABLE OF CONTENTS

INTRODUCTION

The game is on the line. All great teams need someone to turn to.

Shooting is one of the fundamental skills of basketball. And many talented shooters have played in the National Basketball Association (NBA) over the years. They could score from any area of the court. And they often did so with picture-perfect technique.

The greatest shooters have ice running through their veins, though. They can score in bunches. But they can also hit the big shots when it matters most. Those are the shooters that fans never forget.

Here are some of the best shooters in NBA history.

JERRY WEST

Fans have noted that the NBA logo looks an awful lot like Jerry West. The NBA does not say whether West inspired the logo. But if so, it would be a fitting tribute to one of the greatest all-around guards to play the game. West was a brilliant defender, passer, and ball-handler. He was also the best shooter in the NBA for most of his 14 seasons.

West was known for having one of the purest jump shots ever seen. And he could hit from anywhere on the court. That shooting ability helped him win an Olympic gold medal with Team USA in 1960. He then took his skills to Los Angeles. West played his entire career for the Los Angeles Lakers. Later, he served as a successful coach and general manager for the team.

Jerry West, *right*, became a Los Angeles Lakers legend in large part due to his lights-out shooting.

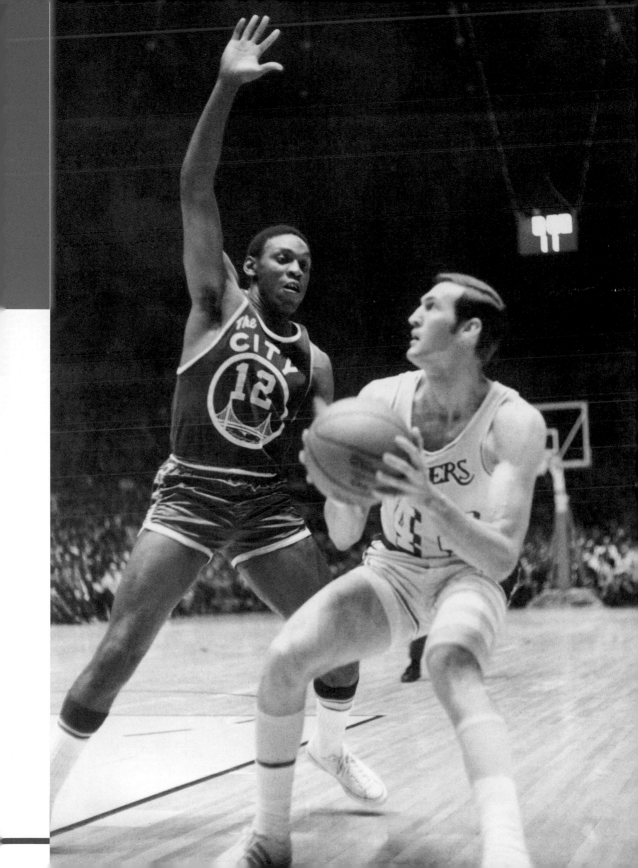

West was a sharpshooter from long range. He retired with 25,192 career points. Only 20 players had scored more through the 2013–14 season. And many of them played after 1979–80. That was the first year the NBA had a three-point line. West was also great at the free-throw line. He made 7,160 foul shots. That ranked sixth all-time through 2013–14.

The Lakers always wanted the ball in West's hands late in games. Perhaps his most famous shot came in a loss. It was Game 3 of the 1970 NBA Finals. The Lakers trailed the New York Knicks by two points. Only seconds remained. That is when West threw up a desperate shot from his own foul line. Shockingly, the ball swished through the hoop on the other end of the court. These days, the shot would have scored three points. Alas, West's shot only counted for two. The Lakers lost in overtime.

840

The number of free throws Jerry West made in 1965–66, an NBA record through 2014.

Lakers guard Jerry West sets up a shot against the New York Knicks during the 1973 NBA Finals.

JERRY WEST

Position: Guard

Hometown: Chelyan, West Virginia

College: West Virginia University

Height, Weight: 6 feet 2, 175 pounds

Birth Date: May 28, 1938

Team: Los Angeles Lakers (1960–74)

All-Star Games: 14 (1961–74)

First-Team All-NBA: 1961–62, 1962–63, 1963–64, 1964–65, 1965–66, 1966–67, 1969–70, 1970–71, 1971–72, 1972–73

KAREEM ABDUL-JABBAR

Some shots are hard to defend. But Kareem Abdul-Jabbar's signature skyhook was nearly impossible to defend. The center stood 7 feet 2 inches tall. He released his one-handed hook shot high above his head. Blocking it was out of the question.

Abdul-Jabbar was born as Lew Alcindor. He changed his name in 1971 when he converted to Islam. The big center was one of basketball's most dominant players for more than two decades. And the skyhook was a big reason for that. The University of California, Los Angeles (UCLA) won three national titles during his time there. Abdul-Jabbar later won six NBA titles over 20 seasons. He was also still the NBA's all-time scoring leader through 2014.

When center Kareem Abdul-Jabbar set up a skyhook, it usually meant two points for his Los Angeles Lakers.

Abdul-Jabbar was tall. But he was also quick, strong, smart, and creative. And he could usually find a weakness in his opponents. Sometimes he used footwork and low-post moves to beat them. Sometimes he used his height to shoot over them. And sometimes he simply bulldozed right through them. But the one weapon he always used was the skyhook.

The skyhook was born when Abdul-Jabbar was in fifth grade. It was a simple hook shot. But Abdul-Jabbar's mastery of the shot earned it a nickname when he got to the NBA. He could use it from anywhere inside the paint. And as his career went on, he started taking the shot from farther out. He usually made it, too.

"It was the only shot I could shoot that didn't get smashed back in my face," Abdul-Jabbar said of his childhood days on the court. "So I learned to rely on it early, and it was always something that I could get off, even in traffic."

38,387

The total number of points Kareem Abdul-Jabbar scored in his career, an NBA record.

The Lakers' Kareem Abdul-Jabbar shoots his skyhook over Boston Celtics defenders in 1988.

KAREEM ABDUL-JABBAR

Position: Center

Hometown: New York, New York

College: UCLA

Height, Weight: 7 feet 2, 225 pounds

Birth Date: April 16, 1947

Teams: Milwaukee Bucks (1969–75)
Los Angeles Lakers (1975–89)

All-Star Games: 19 (1970–77, 1979–89)

MVP Awards: 1970–71, 1971–72, 1973–74, 1975–76,
1976–77, 1979–80

First-Team All-NBA: 1970–71, 1971–72, 1972–73, 1973–74,
1975–76, 1976–77, 1979–80, 1980–81, 1983–84,
1985–86

GEORGE GERVIN

George Gervin got his "Iceman" nickname for a few reasons. One was his clutch shooting. Another was his calmness. Gervin never seemed to be bothered by anything on the court. He said he did not sweat much, either. So people said he had ice in his veins. Hall of Famer Jerry West had high praise for Gervin.

"He's the one player I would pay to see," West said.

Gervin was a cool customer. He was one of basketball's most colorful players for 14 seasons. Gervin began his professional career in the American Basketball Association (ABA). That league merged with the NBA in 1976. Throughout his career, Gervin was known for his smooth and quick release on his jump shot.

The San Antonio Spurs' George Gervin scores on a dunk against the Portland Trail Blazers in 1978.

Gervin rarely took three-pointers, though. Instead, he picked apart defenses inside the arc. And it worked. Gervin led the NBA in scoring four times. He was also the first guard to win three straight NBA scoring titles. Plus, he scored at least 10 points in 407 consecutive games.

63

The number of points George Gervin scored on the final day of the 1978 season. He needed 58 to clinch the scoring title.

Although he was a great outside shooter, Gervin's trademark shot was his finger roll. He started using it after breaking his wrist trying to block a shot. The injury made it hurt to dunk the ball. So instead he would drive toward the basket. Then he would leap high and roll the ball off his fingertips toward the hoop. That shot was more effective than a layup against taller defenders. And Gervin mastered it over his career. He could eventually make it when jumping from as far away as the foul line.

George "The Iceman" Gervin could score at will with his sharp jump shot or his signature finger roll.

GEORGE GERVIN

Position: Guard-Forward

Hometown: Detroit, Michigan

College: Eastern Michigan University

Height, Weight: 6 feet 7, 180 pounds

Birth Date: April 27, 1952

Teams: Virginia Squires (1972–74)
    San Antonio Spurs (1974–85)*
    Chicago Bulls (1985–86)

All-Star Games: 12 (1974–85)*

First-Team All-NBA: 1977–78, 1978–79, 1979–80, 1980–81,
    1981–82

*Stats from 1976 and earlier are from the ABA.

17

LARRY BIRD

Fans today still talk about the 1988 NBA Slam Dunk Contest. Michael Jordan out-dunked Dominique Wilkins in an epic battle. But that was not the only great skills competition showdown that weekend. Larry Bird also put on a show for the ages in that year's Three-Point Shootout.

In the Shootout, players have one minute to take 25 shots from around the three-point arc. Bird won the first two rounds. He did not say a word to his competitors between rounds.

"They know who the favorite is," the Boston Celtics' forward said, "so I really don't have to go in there and say much to anybody."

Boston Celtics legend Larry Bird could hit shots from all over the court during his heyday in the 1980s.

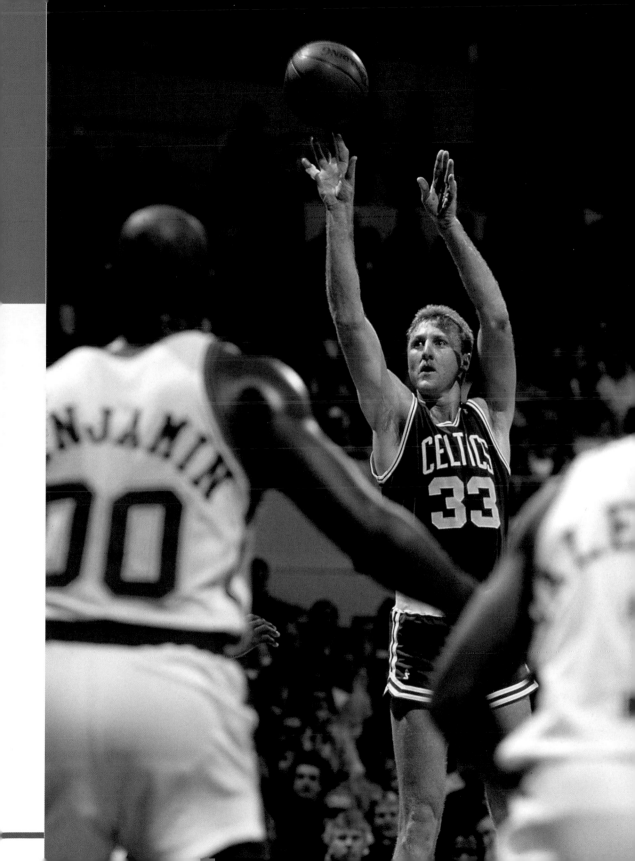

Dale Ellis was not intimidated, though. Like Bird, Ellis was one of the game's purest shooters. When he met Bird in the finals, Ellis opened the round by scoring 15. That put the pressure on Bird. But Bird thrived under pressure. He won three NBA titles in his career. He was also the league's Most Valuable Player (MVP) three times. And he twice led the league in three-pointers made. So Bird went to work. He beat Ellis 17–15.

"I was really concentrating on the two-point balls this year," he said, referring to the last ball in each of the five racks, which counted as two points instead of one. "If you go out there and miss your first three shots on the rack, you can make up for it by making the last shots."

3

The number of NBA titles, league MVP Awards, and Three-Point Shootouts Larry Bird won in his Hall of Fame career.

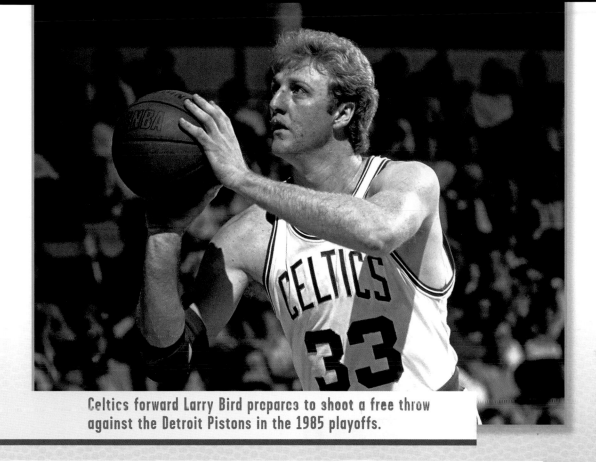

Celtics forward Larry Bird prepares to shoot a free throw against the Detroit Pistons in the 1985 playoffs.

LARRY BIRD

Position: Forward

Hometown: French Lick, Indiana

College: Indiana State University

Height, Weight: 6 feet 9, 220 pounds

Birth Date: December 7, 1956

Team: Boston Celtics (1979–92)

All-Star Games: 12 (1980–88, 1990–92)

MVP Awards: 1983–84, 1984–85, 1985–86

First-Team All-NBA: 1979–80, 1980–81, 1981–82, 1982–83, 1983–84, 1984–85, 1985–86, 1986–87, 1987–88

Three-Point Shootout wins: 1986, 1987, 1988

MICHAEL JORDAN

Michael Jordan dominated the NBA like few players before or since. He won 10 scoring titles. He led his Chicago Bulls to six championships. And he won five MVP Awards. Jordan excelled in many areas. His dunks were spectacular. His defense was fierce. And his leadership was superb. As for his shooting? Well, even Jordan admitted he was not a great shooter early in his career.

It was the part of the game he worked on the most. It paid off. After a few seasons, Jordan was as good as anyone from long range.

Jordan won his first scoring title in his third year in the NBA. He averaged a career-high 37.1 points in that 1986–87 season. Then he won six more scoring titles in a row. Yet, Jordan was often at his best in the postseason.

Michael Jordan takes an off-balance shot for the Chicago Bulls late in a 1989 playoff game against the New York Knicks.

He led the league in postseason scoring 10 times. His best individual postseason might have been 1992–93. Jordan played in 19 games and averaged 35.1 points. The Bulls went on to complete their first championship three-peat. They won another three titles in a row in 1996, 1997, and 1998.

Jordan was of average height for a shooting guard. But he was strong and quick. He could hit long-range jump shots. Or he could slash to the hoop for easy buckets. And with the game on the line, he almost always hit the key shot.

Perhaps his most memorable basket was his last with the Bulls. Jordan faked out a Utah Jazz defender. Then he tossed up the championship-clinching shot from just inside the arc. Jordan left his right arm extended after the shot. The image is now iconic of Jordan's sixth and final title.

6

The number of NBA Finals MVP Awards Michael Jordan won. That was twice as many as any other player through 2013.

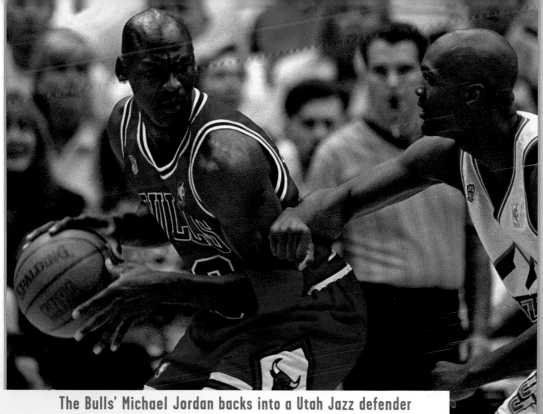

The Bulls' Michael Jordan backs into a Utah Jazz defender during the 1997 NBA Finals.

MICHAEL JORDAN

Position: Shooting guard

Hometown: Wilmington, North Carolina

College: University of North Carolina

Height, Weight: 6 feet 6, 195 pounds

Birth Date: February 17, 1963

Teams: Chicago Bulls (1984–93, 1995–98)
Washington Wizards (2001–03)

All-Star Games: 14 (1985–93, 1996–98, 2002–03)

MVP Awards: 1987–88, 1990–91, 1991–92, 1995–96, 1997–98

First-Team All-NBA: 1986–87, 1987–88, 1988–89, 1989–90, 1990–91, 1991–92, 1992–93, 1995–96, 1996–97, 1997–98

25

CHRIS MULLIN

Chris Mullin grew up playing basketball on the playgrounds of New York. He had a built-in advantage over the other kids. Mullin was left-handed. The others were not used to defending against a lefty. So Mullin took advantage. Those playground games helped him develop into one of the best left-handed shooters in NBA history.

Of course, Mullin could make shots with his right hand, too. You do not make it to the Basketball Hall of Fame without being able to use both sides. But it was that pure left-handed stroke that made him famous.

The Golden State Warriors' Chris Mullin goes up for a shot against the San Antonio Spurs in a 1997 game.

Mullin played on the 1992 US Olympic basketball team. Other "Dream Team" players claimed Mullin was the squad's best shooter. And that team included superstars such as Michael Jordan and Larry Bird. Gail Goodrich was another Hall of Fame left-handed player. He too had high praise for Mullin.

"Some guys just have a knack for finding the ball, have a knack for getting open, and a knack for putting the ball in the basket, and that's Chris Mullin," Goodrich said.

Mullin did not often miss from the free throw line, either. He was a career 86.5 percent free-throw shooter. In 1997–98, he made 93.9 percent of his foul shots. That was the best percentage in the NBA. And it was still the tenth-best percentage through 2014.

Mullin was not just a shooter, though. He was also a fine passer and a tireless worker. Friends used to call him "Gym Rat." He always seemed to be in the gym training. The practice paid off.

3,346

Chris Mullin's NBA-leading minutes played in 1991–92. Mullin also led the NBA in minutes played in 1990–91, with 3,315.

Chris Mullin of the Indiana Pacers looks to pass during a 1997 game against the Washington Wizards.

CHRIS MULLIN

Position: Forward-Guard

Hometown: New York, New York

College: St. John's University

Height, Weight: 6 feet 6, 200 pounds

Birth Date: July 30, 1963

Teams: Golden State Warriors (1985–97, 2000–01)
Indiana Pacers (1997–2000)

All-Star Games: 5 (1989–93)

First-Team All-NBA: 1991–92

MARK PRICE

Any basketball team trailing late in a game looks to get the ball to its best shooter. Defenders just hoped that shooter was not Mark Price.

Getting the ball to Price was an easy choice. He was a great ball-handler. So coaches were confident he would not lose control. He was also a great passer. Price averaged at least 7.0 assists per game in seven consecutive seasons. But most importantly Price was a deadly shooter. He could make shots from all over the court. Defenders guarded him as closely as possible. But that strategy had its pitfalls, too. The tight defense led to many fouls. And Price was practically automatic at the line.

Cleveland Cavaliers guard Mark Price drives to the hoop against the Boston Celtics during a 1992 playoff game.

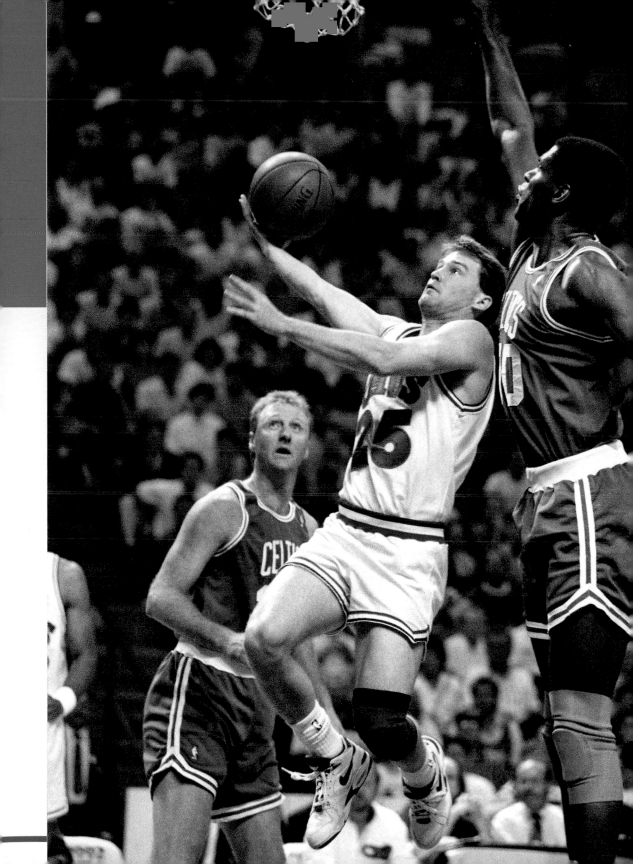

Price made 77 free throws in a row in 1993. He led the NBA in foul-shooting percentage three times. And his career mark was 90.4 percent. Only Steve Nash had a better career free-throw percentage through 2014.

"Good free-throw shooters shoot the same way every time," Price said. "What you want to do is simplify the stroke."

Price was more than just a foul-shooting wizard, though. He was often among the league leaders in field goals and three-pointers. His career three-point percentage was in the top 25 when he retired.

Price was passionate about his craft. When he retired, he started a shooting lab in Suwanee, Georgia. Many pro players used the lab to sharpen their skills. Price also wrote a book called *The Shooter's Touch*.

Price's brother, Brent, also played in the NBA. He didn't shoot as well as his brother. Then again, few players did.

48.7

The percentage of three-point shots Price made in the 1987–88 season. Through 2014, that was the eleventh-best mark in NBA history.

The Cavaliers' Mark Price drives around a Chicago Bulls defender during the 1992 playoffs.

MARK PRICE

Position: Point guard

Hometown: Enid, Oklahoma

College: Georgia Tech

Height, Weight: 6 feet, 170 pounds

Birth Date: February 15, 1964

Teams: Cleveland Cavaliers (1986–95)
 Washington Bullets (1996)
 Golden State Warriors (1996–97)
 Orlando Magic (1997–98)

All-Star Games: 4 (1989, 1992–94)

First-Team All-NBA: 1992–93

Three-Point Shootout wins: 1993, 1994

REGGIE MILLER

Indiana Pacers guard Reggie Miller never met a shot he did not want to take. He fired up shots from all corners of the court. And he often made them.

Miller built a Hall of Fame career on his shooting. He twice led the NBA in three-pointers. And he once held the NBA record for them. Yet Miller might not even have been the best basketball player in his family. His sister, Cheryl Miller, was one of the best women's players ever. She won an Olympic gold medal and two college national titles in the 1980s.

Reggie Miller had a thin frame. But he did not let that take away from his game. He often drove to the hoop. He would challenge much larger defenders. And his step-back move was straight out of a basketball textbook. It gave Miller just enough room for his jump shot.

Indiana Pacers guard Reggie Miller scores on the New York Knicks in the final seconds of their 1995 playoff thriller.

Miller always seemed to play his best against the New York Knicks.
He especially loved playing at Madison Square Garden in New York City. Movie director and Knicks fan Spike Lee often sits courtside at the Garden. He would taunt Miller when the Pacers were in town. And Miller would taunt Lee right back. Miller spoke loudest with his shooting, though.

That showed during the 1995 playoffs. The Knicks were leading Miller's Pacers by six points. Only 16.4 seconds remained. Then Miller drained a three-pointer. Next he stole the in-bounds pass. He dropped back to the three-point line and sank an open three. The game was tied. A few seconds later, Miller grabbed a rebound. He capped off the win with two free throws.

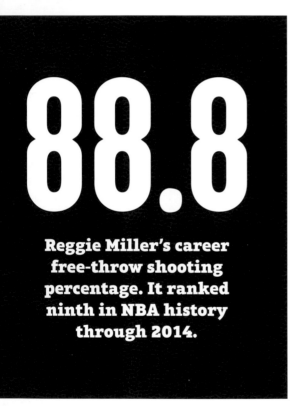

88.8

Reggie Miller's career free-throw shooting percentage. It ranked ninth in NBA history through 2014.

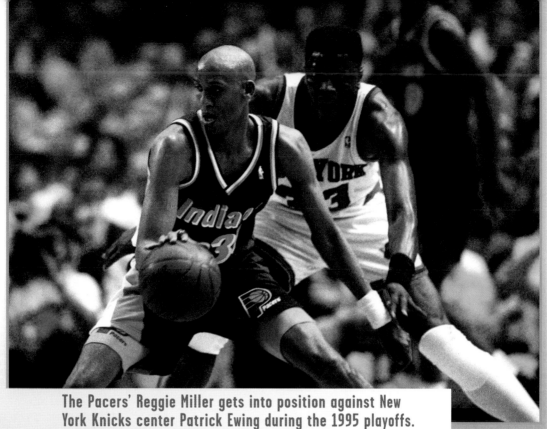

The Pacers' Reggie Miller gets into position against New York Knicks center Patrick Ewing during the 1995 playoffs.

REGGIE MILLER

Position: Shooting guard

Hometown: Riverside, California

College: UCLA

Height, Weight: 6 feet 7, 185 pounds

Birth Date: August 24, 1965

Team: Indiana Pacers (1987–2005)

All-Star Games: 5 (1990, 1995–96, 1998, 2000)

STEVE KERR

Michael Jordan was one of the NBA's all-time dominant scorers. Yet even he trusted Steve Kerr to make important shots—even with a championship on the line.

The year was 1997. Kerr had already won that year's Three-Point Shootout. His sharpshooting performance in the NBA Finals was even more impressive. Kerr's Chicago Bulls led the Utah Jazz three games to two. Only seconds remained in the sixth game. That is when Jordan turned to Kerr on the bench.

"He told me to be ready, that I might be taking the shot," Kerr recalled.

Jordan drove toward the hoop and was double-teamed. Kerr was open. True to his word, Jordan passed to Kerr. And Kerr buried his jump shot. Kerr had won the NBA title for the Bulls.

Chicago Bulls guard Steve Kerr launches the game-winning shot against the Utah Jazz in Game 6 of the 1997 NBA Finals.

"The most memorable shot of my life," Kerr said.

Kerr made many great shots in his 15 NBA seasons. Most of them came from downtown. He twice led the league in three-point shooting percentage. And four times he averaged more than 50 percent on three-pointers.

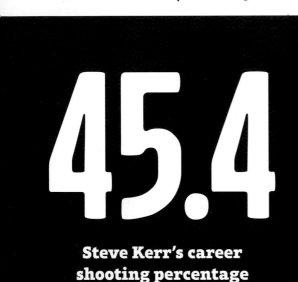

45.4

Steve Kerr's career shooting percentage from three-point range. It was an NBA record through 2014.

Kerr's best weapon was his spot-up jumper. He would find a place on the court away from the ball. He would then stay patient until a teammate was double-teamed. The ball usually came his way soon after. That is the formula Kerr and Jordan used in 1997.

"I said, 'I'll be ready, I'll knock it down,'" Kerr said of his conversation on the bench with Jordan. "He's so good that he draws so much attention. And his excellence gave me the chance to hit the game-winning shot in the NBA Finals. What a thrill."

Steve Kerr celebrates after his shot gave the Bulls the 1997
NBA championship over the Utah Jazz in six games.

STEVE KERR

Position: Point guard

Hometown: Pacific Palisades, California

College: University of Arizona

Height, Weight: 6 feet 3, 175 pounds

Birth Date: September 27, 1965

Teams: Phoenix Suns (1988–89)
    Cleveland Cavaliers (1989–92)
    Orlando Magic (1992–93)
    Chicago Bulls (1993–98)
    San Antonio Spurs (1999–2001, 2002–03)
    Portland Trail Blazers (2001–02)

Three-Point Shootout win: 1997

RAY ALLEN

The Miami Heat's season was on the line. The team had come into the 2013 NBA Finals with high hopes. Yet the players found themselves seconds away from elimination. The San Antonio Spurs led Game 6 by three points. Only a few seconds remained. That is when Heat center Chris Bosh passed the ball to the NBA's greatest three-point shooter ever.

Ray Allen was waiting in the corner. He set his feet. He took the pass. Then he jumped into the air and released a picture-perfect jumper. *Swish.*

The game was tied. Miami went on to win in overtime. Then the Heat took the series in Game 7.

"It's going to be a shot that I'm going to remember for a long time," Allen said.

Miami Heat guard Ray Allen hits the last-second, game-tying three-pointer in Game 6 of the 2013 NBA Finals.

Teams have been calling on Allen to make three-pointers for nearly two decades. The Milwaukee Bucks traded for Allen before he played an NBA game. He certainly made a lot of triples for the Bucks and others. Through the 2013–14 season, no player had taken more three-point shots. And no player had made more three-pointers, either. Allen had also led the NBA in three-point baskets three times.

Allen's sharpshooting had made him an NBA star. However, he was unable to win a championship in his first 11 years. That finally changed in 2007–08. The Boston Celtics traded for Allen before that season. They also traded for forward Kevin Garnett. The team hoped the veteran stars could help the Celtics reclaim past glory. Allen certainly did his part. He made 22 three-pointers in the NBA Finals. That was a record at the time. It also helped Boston win its first NBA title in 22 seasons.

269

The number of three-pointers Ray Allen made in 2005–06. That was the second-most in NBA history through 2014.

Boston Celtics guard Ray Allen celebrates after hitting a three-pointer in the 2008 NBA Finals.

RAY ALLEN

Position: Shooting guard

Hometown: Dalzell, South Carolina

College: University of Connecticut

Height, Weight: 6 feet 5, 205 pounds

Birth Date: July 20, 1975

Teams: Milwaukee Bucks (1996–2003)
Seattle SuperSonics (2003–07)
Boston Celtics (2007–12)
Miami Heat (2012–)

All-Star Games: 10 (2000–02, 2004–09, 2011)

Three-Point Shootout win: 2001

STEVE NASH

Canada produces thousands of great hockey players. Steve Nash chose a different path. The British Columbia native was a standout on the basketball court. In college at Santa Clara University, he became a rare All-American from Canada. In the NBA, he put together a career that will likely be honored in the Hall of Fame.

Few players in NBA history have had Nash's all-around skill set. He is a fantastic passer and dribbler. He is a tireless worker. Plus, Nash also happens to be a great shooter. Together, those skills work like a charm. Defenders who try to stop Nash's passing get burned by his shot. Those who try to stop his shot get burned by his playmaking.

Steve Nash of the Phoenix Suns launches a three-pointer against the San Antonio Spurs during a 2006 game.

Nash knows how to run an offense.

Through 2014, the point guard had led the NBA in total assists six times. But he had also made more than half of his two-point field goals 11 times. It is rare for guards to shoot such a high percentage. Meanwhile, Nash had made more than 40 percent of his three-pointers in 14 different seasons. And he had made 90.4 percent of his free throws through the 2013–14 season. That was an NBA record.

Nash was at his best during his second stint with the Phoenix Suns. He won the MVP Award in 2004–05 and 2005–06. He made more than half of his shots and more than 43 percent of his three-pointers in both seasons. During that first MVP season, he averaged 15.5 points and 11.5 assists per game. The next season, he averaged 18.8 points and 10.5 assists per game. Plus, he made a league-best 92.1 percent of his foul shots.

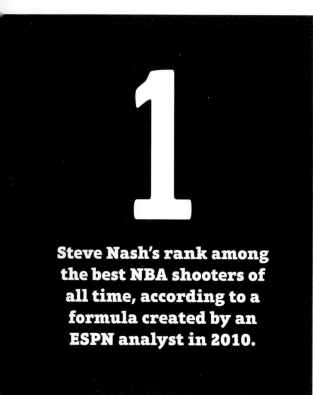

1

Steve Nash's rank among the best NBA shooters of all time, according to a formula created by an ESPN analyst in 2010.

The Suns' Steve Nash hits a jump shot late in a 2006 playoff game against the Los Angeles Clippers.

STEVE NASH

Position: Point guard

Hometown: Victoria, British Columbia, Canada

College: Santa Clara University

Height, Weight: 6 feet 3, 195 pounds

Birth Date: February 7, 1974

Teams: Phoenix Suns (1996–98, 2004–12)
Dallas Mavericks (1998–2004)
Los Angeles Lakers (2012–)

All-Star Games: 8 (2002–03, 2005–08, 2010, 2012)

MVP Awards: 2004–05, 2005–06

First-Team All-NBA: 2004–05, 2005–06, 2006–07

DIRK NOWITZKI

European basketball players are known for their fundamentals. That focus has helped create some great shooters. The best of those European shooters might be 7-footer Dirk Nowitzki of Germany.

Power forwards usually play close to the basket. But the Dallas Mavericks' star can hit his shots from the inside to beyond the three-point arc. That makes guarding him a nightmare. He has been the centerpiece for many great Mavericks teams, including the 2011 NBA champions. The soft-shooting big man was named the Finals MVP.

Nowitzki came by his basketball ability naturally. His mom played basketball for the women's national team in West Germany. His father was a star in team handball. That sport combines many of the talents needed to play hoops.

Dallas Mavericks forward Dirk Nowitzki showed that 7-footers can make three-pointers.

Young Dirk was drawn to his mom's sport. His excellence was soon obvious. The Milwaukee Bucks picked Nowitzki ninth overall in the 1998 NBA Draft. However, they immediately traded him to the Mavericks. That turned out to be a big mistake.

Nowitzki has been lights-out since joining the NBA. He has averaged at least 20 points per game in 13 of his 16 seasons through 2014. He is usually among the league leaders in shooting and scoring. Plus, he won the 2006–07 MVP Award.

Any questions about Nowitzki's greatness were answered in the 2011 NBA Finals. He came into Game 2 with a badly injured middle finger on his left hand. Yet Nowitzki scored the Mavericks' final nine points in a 95–93 win. And he scored two of those baskets with his left hand. That showed he is not only smooth, but tough.

582

The number of points Dirk Nowitzki scored in the postseason on his way to the 2011 NBA title. No player scored more in those playoffs.

The Mavericks' Dirk Nowitzki shoots against the Sacramento Kings during a 2014 game.

DIRK NOWITZKI

Position: Power forward

Hometown: Wurzburg, Germany

High School: Rontgen Gymnasium

Height, Weight: 7 feet, 237 pounds

Birth Date: June 19, 1978

Team: Dallas Mavericks (1999–)

All-Star Games: 12 (2002–12, 2014)

MVP Award: 2006–07

First-Team All-NBA: 2004–05, 2005–06, 2006–07, 2008–09

Three-Point Shootout win: 2006

KEVIN DURANT

LeBron James and Paul George are two of the NBA's best defensive players. Both were asked whom they had the toughest time guarding. And both quickly answered: Kevin Durant.

Durant stands at 6 feet 9 inches. Players of that height usually score most of their points close to the hoop. Durant is not one of them. He led the NBA in total points every season from 2009–10 to 2013–14. And he did so by hitting shots from everywhere. Many of his baskets were three-pointers. And a lot of his points came from the free-throw line. Durant led the league in total free throws in each of those five seasons. That helped Durant have the NBA's highest scoring average four times during that span.

Oklahoma City Thunder forward Kevin Durant won four NBA scoring titles from 2009–10 to 2013–14.

Fans knew of Durant's talent from his college days. But when he first came to the NBA as a shooting guard, he was inconsistent. Then Scott Brooks took over as coach of the Oklahoma City Thunder in 2008–09. He moved Durant to small forward. Durant went from being a great scorer to an NBA scoring champion. He also helped turn the Thunder into winners. They had lost a team record 62 games in 2007–08. Four years later, the Thunder reached the 2012 NBA Finals.

Durant has had many great scoring nights. On January 18, 2013, he put up a career-high 52 points. That included a 21-for-21 night from the free-throw line. Only one player had made more free throws in a game without a miss through 2014.

Almost exactly one year later, Durant set a new career high. He scored 54 points against the Golden State Warriors on January 17, 2014.

849

The number of field goals Durant made in 2013–14. That was a career high and also the NBA high for that season.

The Thunder's Kevin Durant drives to the basket during a 2014 game against the San Antonio Spurs.

KEVIN DURANT

Position: Small forward

Hometown: Seat Pleasant, Maryland

College: University of Texas

Height, Weight: 6 feet 9, 215 pounds

Birth Date: September 29, 1988

Teams: Seattle SuperSonics/Oklahoma City Thunder (2007–)

All-Star Games: 5 (2010–14)

First-Team All-NBA: 2009–10, 2010–11, 2011–12, 2012–13

STEPHEN
CURRY

Dell Curry was one of the NBA's sharpest shooters for 16 seasons. He taught his son to be even better. Golden State Warriors guard Stephen Curry developed into one of the best pure shooters in the NBA.

The younger Curry developed his shot with his dad. In high school, Stephen shot from the hip. But Dell thought Stephen's unique form might limit his future. So together they worked on the more traditional shooting form.

"All summer when I was at camps people were like, 'Who are you, why are you playing basketball?'" Curry said. "I was really that bad for a month and a half [before] I finally figured it out."

It might have taken a while, but he finally got comfortable with his new form. And his new shot became unstoppable.

Golden State Warriors guard Stephen Curry hits a three-pointer against the Chicago Bulls in 2014.

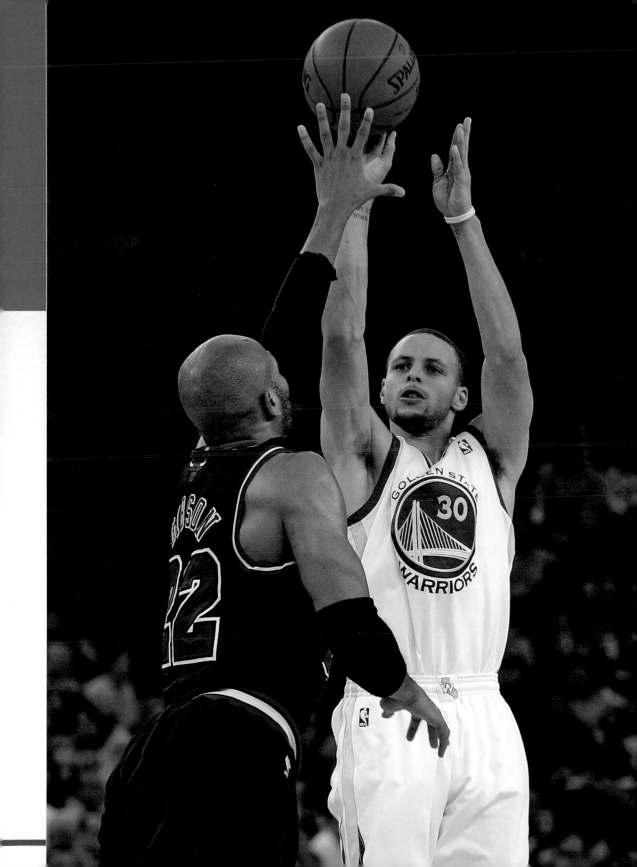

Curry went on to play at Davidson College in North Carolina. There he became an All-American and the best shooter in the country. The Warriors then picked him in the first round of the 2009 NBA Draft.

Curry did not miss a beat as a pro. His coaches let him fire away from wherever he saw fit. And he rarely misses when he has time to set himself for a shot. In 2012–13 and 2013–14, Curry led the league in both three-pointers and three-point attempts. But he also can hit pull-ups, step-backs, and running shots. It is no wonder why the Warriors soon developed one of the NBA's top offenses.

.934

Stephen Curry's free-throw percentage in 2010–11. It was an NBA best.

"I've never played with someone who can shoot it like Steph," former Warriors guard Jarrett Jack said. "He's the best shooter at his position by far."

The Warriors' Stephen Curry prepares to shoot a free throw during a 2014 game against the Phoenix Suns.

STEPHEN CURRY

Position: Point guard

Hometown: Charlotte, North Carolina

College: Davidson College

Height, Weight: 6 feet 3, 185 pounds

Birth Date: March 14, 1988

Team: Golden State Warriors (2009–)

All-Star Game: 1 (2014)

HONORABLE MENTIONS

Paul Arizin – In the 1950s, when the jump shot was just becoming a weapon, Arizin was the master. The longtime Philadelphia Warriors small forward twice led the NBA in scoring.

Rick Barry – As smooth a shooter as basketball has seen, Barry twice made 1,000 field goals in a season during the 1960s and 1970s.

Kobe Bryant – No one has hit more big shots in recent years than the Los Angeles Lakers' star, even with two or three defenders on him. Bryant has led the league in points four times through 2014.

Dale Ellis – Ellis made 100 or more three-pointers in nine different seasons and hit a league-best 46.4 percent in 1997–98. He also won the 1989 Three-Point Shootout.

Jeff Hornacek – The fearless shooter for the Phoenix Suns and the Utah Jazz was among the top five in three-point shooting in five seasons during the 1990s.

Sam Jones – Jones was the guy who the championship Boston Celtics of the 1950s and 1960s always wanted taking the big shot.

Glen Rice – One of the first great shooting forwards from three-point land, Rice won the 1995 Three-Point Shootout and six times was in the top 10 in three-pointers made.

Bill Sharman – The shooting guard won four NBA titles during 11 seasons spent mostly with the Celtics and was considered one of the greatest outside shooters of the 1950s and 1960s.

John Stockton – Known for his assists—he was the NBA career leader through 2014—Stockton also was a sharpshooter, especially on three-pointers, for the Utah Jazz in the 1990s.

Peja Stojakovic – A great long-range shooter from Croatia, Stojakovic also led the league in free-throw shooting two times and won two Three-Point Shootouts.

GLOSSARY

assist
A pass that leads directly to a basket.

blocked shot
A play in which a shooter's field goal attempt is knocked down by a defender before it can reach the rim.

draft
A system used by professional sports leagues to spread incoming talent throughout all of the teams.

hook shot
A one-handed shot taken from over the head.

paint
Also known as the free-throw lane, this is the area under the hoop. Sometimes this space is painted over with a solid color.

rebound
A recovery of a missed shot.

rookie
A first-year player in the NBA.

veteran
A player with a lot of experience.

FOR MORE INFORMATION

Further Readings

Silverman, Drew. *Basketball*. Minneapolis, MN: Abdo Publishing Co., 2012.

Silverman, Drew. *The NBA Finals*. Minneapolis, MN: Abdo Publishing Co., 2013.

Websites

To learn more about NBA's Best Ever, visit **booklinks.abdopublishing.com**. These links are routinely monitored and updated to provide the most current information available.

INDEX

ABOUT THE AUTHOR

Barry Wilner has been a sportswriter for The Associated Press since 1976. He has written about every sport and has covered every Super Bowl since 1985. He has also covered every FIFA World Cup since 1986, the Stanley Cup Finals, the Summer and Winter Olympics, the Pan American Games, championship boxing matches, plus major golf and tennis tournaments. He has written more than 40 books.